In the Mixed Gender of the Sea

Jennifer MacPherson

Table of Contents

Part One

Part Two

Part Three

This one's for Frank... he knows the reasons

I

In The Mixed Gender Of The Sea

Because we become whom we love,
I shiver in an attic room, my knees
grates of ivory iron. Although you are not here,
I see your eyes, splashes of blue color
when the sky hazes over before thunder,
before storms, before the scorch from lightning.

> *rain smoothes you out like bottle glass*
> *your hair a bright banner*
> *winds bear you north while I go south*
> *you are not cold   but lonely*
> *were you ever green   ever a fire?*

Because we become whom we love,
I reluctantly float up chimneys like heavy smoke,
beat against this rocky shore and try to change
the coastline's shape. It will never change.
And I curse my own knowledge:
I would not love it nearly as much if it did.

> *you bob like a cork in the sea   a cork in the sea*
> *winds bear you east while I go west*
> *you wear your smoke like a coat*
> *but if you were a pyre*
> *you would not burn   would never burn.*

so I have returned to this landlocked plot,
this barren, restless house where my pulse beats white
and I waken to wet sheets. In my dreaming, my torso
lengthens in the dawn, my hair streams like marsh grass,
my body curves into coves at low tide,
I breathe salt and become whom I love.

Varieties of Light

Where did it come from, your first astonishment?
From my mother's tight shoulder,
from the roughness of stones on a summer's day.
I don't remember if there was sun;
my mother's nipples ran with poison.
I tasted war and my father's last kiss.

When did you first study the stars' bright hours?
How does one measure the shadows
thrown by comets, their stop at each station?
That is how long, both the coming and the stop,
and the length of their shadow at first light.
They are fine-stemmed flowers that will never wilt.

Did you swallow roses,
walk out slowly on the limb of chance?
Limbs break easily at the beginning of dusk
and roses fold their cups of light.
I am enough a child of chance to want
no more of it. I came to you.

Will you meet me again tomorrow,
let me drink from your wrists,
your anklebones? I have lived where I
wore no shoes, where I forgot the lull of food.
I ate my dress like bread
but you are welcome to its buttons.

Will your bones blend into the night
while you sleep? Will your light disappear?
I don't know about sleep or blood's
dominion. Bring soil tomorrow
and we will plant lupine and sweet pea,
scatter all our seeds of desire.

Proposal of Marriage

In Australia I saw
a million bats in trees
above the Alligator River.
They made a dreadful rustling

as they roosted like long leaves
drooping from branches
so thick
they closed out the sky.

I couldn't imagine
them flying through my house
one by one although I knew
they could, my "yes" a snake's hiss.

What was the promise
I wanted?
Spring or maybe raging waters
with morning toast and

at day's end,
a tidy fire in the grate,
night held
close in its insignificant arms.

A Short History of Red

Carmine of cheek
slapped by an angry mother,
rouge put on
perhaps under a little powder,
lips to match:
napkin's subtle kiss.

June's peonies:
cups running over with redness
late for the season and falling over the fence,
the sun sipping light from these cups
reflecting every coral flower

Scarlet dress
shoes to match
no back, mostly cleavage in front:
a dare for walks in the dark alley

Autumn's boisterous sports car
horn blaring.
The driver's tossed scarf and glove,
scuffle of leaves they land in,
disappear:
russet camouflage.

This is a red land we live in, my love
nothing redder than desire.
Toss my scarf onto the fire's blaze:
dress, blossom, sun, flesh and kiss.
Watch the year burn.

Mangoes and Honey

Let their bodies roll and kick,
slide against each other, twin minks
sucking each other's fur.
They are lying on torn rags, clothes
they discarded when their fire began its howl.
Her mouth puckers. How sweetly
she commands, "Fuck me. Give me
your torch, your silky hammer,
all of your love-sap," And he
answers her, calls her ""Bitch" and "Blossom,"
says her skin is smooth as mango.

Let the man scream when he comes,.
Let the woman pant under a yolk- mooned sky
beads of sweat like globes of honey
dropped by errant bees. It's steamy-hot,
the woman moaning and all those sweet
winged things flying in circles,
dizzy and full. Paths of honey
trace between her breasts. The man
is a bear snuffling for sweets.
All, all are here.

Physical Examination

There is a gum-ball machine in my head
and a jukebox stuck on "Light My Fire."

My feet try to hurry, stuck in their snowshoes.
The bear in me demands to be filled.

Freezer-burn scars my toes
but my wrists are catalogs of hope.

I could see sleep in anyone's eyes.
I could feel love in the shape of a skull.

Perfect & Invisible

like love gone green-apple sour
or worse, gone slack like its soft sister,

like pain mellowing into forgotten slumber,
an ache that remembers the good years,

like the hard worm of grief,
eater of silk and harsh history,

like desire in all its milk or passion's poppy
that sways and sways at a touch,

like anger's ocean and river,
its torrential niagara, the boat lost in the fog,

like hope hanging on, tattered
moth with orange wing.

What Is Hidden

eyes   voice
the act behind the door

pendant tucked between breasts
candy tucked behind tongue

the key that opens desire
These   and more as well

spill their shadows on the sidewalk
write their story where no one can read it

I want his eyes to be open
when we love

his voice
to bell in tones that leave me deaf

I want the tongue not the candy
breasts crushed against his chest

I want the key turned and lost
shining in his eyes

Desire

could be water
a pool the temperature of flesh

the waterfall that touches your shoulder

the cascade down the water-slide as you hit the flat surface
but it's not flat anymore, it's roiling

and the little boat is tossing and you're flung
yes, you're flung out into that maelstrom

but, really
it's gentle and pulses against your skin.

Your world inside
that secret place where you are strong
melts.

No One Pities the Hopeful

Imagine a pint
of Godiva white chocolate raspberry ice cream,
how it conjures up visions
of sinful richness, dim living room
speckled by candles,
Casablanca's
few hours of rented nostalgia,
sweet treats
proud and dreaming
of long spoons.
Alas for the anonymous dinner,
the undressed salad,
the bologna sandwich.
Instead, consider the banana,
its erotic connotation
at breakfast.

when I have no lover and the sky is a rootless tree hung with tiny lamps

The house shines, the sky a melting pot.
A sudden longing for pesto
swoops through me
like a roller coaster on fire.

Crispest sprigs of basil,
seven rose-tipped cloves,
olive oil and salt.
Whip, blend. Whip, blend.

My face pressed close
I can smell their pungent flame:
pesto fit for Aphrodite
searing love into flesh.

A little pasta, a little pesto, a little parmesan.
I pile my plate, drag myself
into the crawlspace beneath the stairs
where the air is muffler-warm,

curl up with old luggage,
the burning soles of my boots
and other periodic travelers:
my solitary loves.

Come to my table, I succor with food

Are you in need of care and feeding?
Is your digestion at its sturdy best?
Casseroles are popping in the oven.
Stockpots are splashing up the burners,
and a sizzle of stir-fry's an eyelash away.

Fresh chilies and radish will singe your tongue,
cayenne, curry, garlic, torment your nose.
Those tender spots once safely hidden?
They're exposed now. They gasp and heave,
your sinuses open, your appetite huge.

You will dance with the enchiladas,
spin drunkenly, tostadas for a hat.
Mexico over-runs the flowering garden –
or Poland reigns with hand-rolled pierogi,
kielbasa garlands, babushkas everywhere.

If sweet's your desire, I can dazzle
with dessert: a tart, a torte, a well-baked pie,
eight-layer cakes with caramel crème,
and my warm thighs to tent the bed –
I've a navel guaranteed to drive you wild.

The Tear

ducts
are in rebellion
again
quarts of salt to be mined

and it all costs
nothing
unless we consider
the source of it
the pressure behind the cheekbones
sounds that may (or may not)
choke themselves free.

Pain hangs in the air
though we cannot see it swing.
Its bright flag blooms above the corners
of our mouths.

Our faces have become
shipwrecks
and the crews have gone to lunch.
May this teach us always to wear
scarves.

All, all
from such a tiny
speck
we'd thought too small
to brush away.

Woman As Hawk

The woman
baits hooks all day,
untangles lines.
She watches
the circling hawks,
envies the blank box
of their faces.
She pokes
holes in her thumbs,
sometimes mistaking
her life for the fishhook,
sometimes for bait.
She knows worms
as well as any friend,
intimate
their sleek caress,
their smooth design,
no waste –
just plump desire.

Love's Wound

How the muscles on his back rippled as he bent to her.
She was an arm across his neck, a fall of hair, flames
rising from her scalp like Medusa's snakes.

They walked into golden fire. They wrapped
the world in its fuzzy spring blanket, yellow and green,
a sky of chartreuse rain.

After he opened the letter, it was never the same.
Flowers wilted. His hat
grew grey with dust and he needed

glasses to read the pamphlets that her father sent
with the message: "Return to Jesus,"
though he never remembered leaving.

He waited for the Roadrunner to come with his whirligig,
a feather to tuck behind his ear, a bright scarf
to camouflage his wounds, the ones that showed.

The Longing

She has crawled into the music, mouth agape
in a throaty hum. Her body sways,
transformed with longing to become that drumbeat,
the skin of the drum, that gypsy
guitar, its drunken slides up and down
her nerves a scale of their own.
She drips melody, cheeks and thighs
glistening in moon's gold glimmer. Her hum
takes flight but no one hears this bird, words
locked tight in the silence behind the song.

Kisses 101

I want to tell you about kisses,
Kisses are messy. Not everyone
likes them but no one ever says so
unless it is a nine-year old boy.
Men who are still nine at heart
avoid kissing. Their lips
feel like frogs, their breath
smells of the swamp.

Some men are bad kissers
with no hope of improvement.
No one tells them, so their love life
is a thirsty desert. These are men who
missed the kissing lesson
in dance class. Since girls never
miss dance class, they have no
excuses for bad kisses. They
seldom need them

I like kisses. Always have, though I
was slow to start. Before she learned
the hard lessons of separation, mother
quizzed me. I was sixteen,
shy and unready, unwilling
to confess my inexperience. So began
my series of lies about kissing and
all other important subjects.

Did I kiss and tell about the boys
who waylaid me on dark nights
among tall trees? Did I keep the faith
about broken springs in the Buick's back seat?
Did my mussed hair ever yield
stammered explanation? When I stole a kiss,

whose pot of gold did I plunder? Am I
telling the truth with these paper kisses
or am I only weaving fables
for my trembling tongue's delight?

The Dark Room

At *The Dark Room*, lovers and politicians
crowd the bar for single malt scotches.
sipped in Michelangelo light.

Ten years ago, my black lover
tossed salads and made food look pretty. Tongue busy
with his chef's French or the sibilants of street talk,
he shone fluent where it counted, in the geography
of my body, knew my ankles' swift lock when I came,
the calves' can't-help-it-oh-my-glory clench.

He's gone now. At *The Dark Room*, someone else
curls shreds of carrot and turns parsley into flowers
on salads and croissants. Lean-loined waiters serve
the succulents, their tongues tied with Thai and Yiddish
and seven types of sushi. They suggest oysters to begin
but I don't need them.

In my new lover's bedroom, dark-draped windows
transform his warm-sheeted nest into a black hole
where I couldn't find my clothes even if I wanted to.
We taste each other's salty skin, delight in its brine.
Night's grammar here is Braille in another language.

Desire at Sixty

I covet the long slow ache of love,
how it chastens the body,
how it teaches patience, discourages frenzy,
forces the most exterior act to become interior.

Head-of-the-match blue fire
instead of blazing red.

Eyes open, throat open,
opal moans and diamonds and pearls
not to adorn
but savored and warmed,

bed sheets all smelling of iron and fresh, hot percale.

II

Wolf

I dreamed I kissed a wolf last night.
Blood on his ears, he pointed at blossoms
falling, skies open with bursts of fire,
said the weight of understanding is heavier
than love, that in the chocolate dark, some men
are cowards. They look for motorcycles
to speed out of hell, afraid of dwarfs in trees
or snow geese flying north, anything
they cannot roll between their palms.
They look for a lady to lay their burdens on,
spilling secrets upon her bed sheets
until she is smothered.
Wolves carry pain in their paws, he said:
Come, give me yours

November

There are still days
when coats and jackets can be left
hanging on hooks

when gasps of wind catch us unaware
even now as November
turns its tight corner

and we are seared
by scarves of leaves
our shoulders cannot hold

Her Sister's Wedding Day

Eyes swollen shut with light,
her fingers stroked the bannister's
smooth slide, smells of polish
and lemon soap mixed
with yesterday's pot roast and cabbage.
It was enough
to play outside her bedroom, lilacs
spilling purple blossoms everywhere.

She chewed her sweater cuffs,
their mothball scent tasting
like old sheets in a drawer,
knew today was moving on to church
and ribbon-tied oak pews, to cakes' sweet pain
and garters flying, gasoline and
her sister driving off in that silver car,
the feel of beeswax on her hands.

Gravel Roads

I dream about you, your voice
   an image of flashing lights, vague
      undertones of possible thunder
         in the morning, red sky
            at night. Sailors howl like wolves.

Too literal, too direct, I must
   learn to lean to the side, lean
      out of the moving car as it rounds the curve
         swing out with its heavy door,
            drag my braids in the dust,

the way we rode the station wagon
   when we were kids. After hurricane Diane
      we trolled the dusty
         two-lane roads, sitting on the back flap,
         our sneakers thwacking the gravel

each time the car hit a bump,
   passion a rumble of thunder we only sensed
      dim and far-off, in the night,

evergreen of the Pocono trees yielding
   to smooth rounded farms like
      the shape of a girl emerging from encircling arms.

Twenty Years Apart

I am sure that an angel guided my trips to the market
for food and wine, to the Mall
for high-priced outfits that cradled my hips,
lacy lingerie, Monet prints, bayberry candles --
all the baubles and beads of my life.

When I was closest to fatal longing,
this angel hid the knives
I would have used to pierce my heart
because the life I knew was over.
 I asked this angel if she guarded what I
remembered and she said, "No, I guard your voice."

Now my car drives itself past pizza joints,
New Age bookstores, cafes with exotic names.
In the clamorous past, there was a five-and-dime,
a pawn shop, a barber, and two little Jewish tailors,
voices thick with faded gutterals. One by one,
they disappeared as the 1960's became just a refrain.

Memories perch on my shoulder.
Uneasy angels stir restlessly,
keep contentment lodged in my throat like a knife
that severs my past and leaves me
scathed but singing still.

Replacements

Why do I remember the blue and green print dress
that burned in the clothing store fire
better than the red plaid sheath I bought to replace it?
Why does it remain a dream of sapphire and emerald swirls
even now, though the fire's been out for thirty years?

Why do you lovingly compare each new car
to the '39 Buick you owned for a week when you were
seventeen, before you wrecked it running a red light?
Why do you still dream of the girl who threw you over
for a more muscular man?

Don't we all long for what we just missed having?
Not like becoming a ballerina when you can't walk,
but missing the leap to *prima* from the *corps de ballet*.
The almost made, the might-have-been. The shot that hit
the green then bounced into the water-trap.

So if I murmur another's name at night
when I turn to you, asleep,
it's just that I'm wearing a blue and green dress
that flares each time my partner,
dead ten years now, spins me around in our dance.

And if you dream of a dark haired Italian girl,
and call out her name,
your pillow bruised with yearning,
it's because you spied an ad for a smart new car
that comes with no guarantees.

Dinner Party

when the ladle broke
I caught my breath
a knife skittered off its platter

gravy spelled vesuvius at our table
wreaking havoc
as all the guests scattered

chair legs broke
a vase shattered
noise pooled deep and violent as rabid dogs

it didn't matter
that the goldberg variations
played softly in the other room

or that the chicken ran plump and juicy
air tinged with scents
of caramel and lime

or that a woman languished on a chaise
the shutters closed in a back room
where nobody goes

these stains will never come out
our cats still would have been poisoned
war would have broken out anyway

In Times of Doubt

If I could pour bright parabolas
of cinnamon light over my shoulders

If I could shelter among the burgeoning fruit:
the avocado and pear

If I could bathe, rinsed
with the juice of squeezed lemons,

emerge translucent and Catholic, clean
as philosophy

Dark And Huge And Dusted With Wings

Carrion-eaters circle the courtyard.
My mother holds my little sister's
hand. On her lap, the baby toes are still.

My sister plays dead, eyes sweet and fruity.
Her hand lies near the screens
where bats cling. She is never lonely.

Down the hall, the phone hangs
like a solemn guard. It never has given me
anything I wanted, anything I could carry with me.

But it still hangs there, uniformed in silence,
waiting for the last bird's hot breath.
My sister's eyes have finally closed in sleep.

How our dreams have faltered!
Dry-eyed, I cry among violets and cinnamon.
We are all at drought here.

She Dreams Of A Painting

The moth hovers, envelops lilac
and lily-gold girl, asleep at the piano.

A tiger crouches under the branches
of her smile. She wakens to a hall

of frescoes, Magi and Virgin
adoring. A fountain plays with shadows

in nearby mountains and winds lie calm
between the breasted hills.

Women & Fruit

The men have spent days on their fine yellow
machines, harvesting, calling to children
to toss in those fallen apples and scarified pears.
Each peach reflects a shiny dollar.

Women wave aprons, chant as they march
on the kitchen. Their hair is tied in flags
of bright service. They are not sure of who they are
but they smell the fruit

and know it must be ladled into Ball jars,
or spooned in crusts they roll and crimp, or those tricky
Danish pastries with their butter-brushed layers.
They will fill the pantry.

Some women make pies, others make mischief.
When the fruit turns bad, do they hide their every knife?
Knives can scoop an eye out,
scalp a curly head, bring relief to migraine.

And the women love the shiny steel blades,
black mother-of-pearl handles, have carved their initials
in all the door lintels with the tips. Every woman
needs something she can call her own.

How Your Hands Lay On My Skin

I don't remember losing your address
    in the cluttered map of my purse,
        or possibly in a slipcover's seam.

I don't remember losing my watch, time itself
    burning my wrist.

I don't recall forgetting my last name, only
    remembering yours.

I don't remember moonlight when it wasn't
    falling on your dark body.

I don't remember what you said or I said
    on any particular day.
        Maybe we ate the words in a sandwich.
            Maybe we rubbed them out in your ashtray, all
                the little letters scattered and burned.

I remember how our bodies swayed like palms
    as they joined, washed by the sun
        in the oasis of your sheets.

I knew – but I forgot – all things end in smoke and cinder.

I don't remember the doors closing, just staring
    at their carved figures, their jeweled intaglio;
        I remember pulling at the bell over and over,
            knowing you could not hear it ring.

September Rain

autumn arrives full blast with
spill of sunflower seeds

wind plays tag with leaves but it's no game
it is as serious as your going

where went those summer months of open mouths
beech-light days   nights of inner thunder

ear close to mine   heartbeat
mirroring ocean's swell and spill

rain falling like irish mist until
ground lies sodden and squirrels spin drunk

you walk away through corrupted air
thick grasses snagging your heels

trees heavy with loss
leaves preoccupied with dying

Icicles & Seaweed

afterward you
asked for a poem
you demanded icicles and seaweed
and a cup of green tea

hot cement burned my feet
you broke off icicles to cool them
anointed each toe with the scorpion's bite

of your kiss   oh you are a deadly love
you burn me over and over
falling everywhere
hotter than the cautery of ice

and the largest icicles hang three stories long
thick as a man's thigh
they are pulling off the gables of my roof

look at them fall with
the first thaw   all my defenses
I will have rain on my head forever
and seaweed will steam in the saline of my tears

already I foresee how you will leave me
how you will pull night air behind you like vines of ice
how earth will turn to sea and I a flat rock

Black Ice

lake moxencockie's shore
thick with trees

shelters the bones of old boats
bleached to the beige of oak

I remember when these bones
were new and the waters

shone white like the hills
which were green and covered with roses

maybe memory serves me poorly
and only one rose grew

but it seemed the whole hill
flowered

lilies floated in the water
the possibility of ice a dream

Separate Beds

You never listen when I say
I see your face in every shell
or when I tell you the wind
makes a noose of your collar.
and the sea crashes down your door,
furniture swept out by the churning tide.

I had told you to bind the bolt
with cloth, to tie it tightly – water
understands some bolts cannot
be opened – but you could not hear
any voice but your own.
Now each night howls without you.

My bones bend in the light from candles
we've never lit. I drink wine from bottles,
corks still intact. Wine racks line
the cellar walls. Stacked boxes marked
Dreams Mine, Dreams Yours,
smell of salt. Mice have nibbled them;
their sides gape open, half-collapsed,
but I can see how, inside,
they still shine.

Leavetaking

trumpets of tulips line the steps
their droop clutches
for one more day of flower

trees thin to a fine point
fruit shrivel   listen
to the sizzle of soil as it dries

shadows lurk behind cacti
each one lean as a coyote
on the prowl

when hunger bites my heart
I spill blood but it does not feed me
tears a gift I cannot cry

you were a shiny coin in my desert
now dust covers your shoes and the sun
slants more toward the east

than it used to

A List Of Answers To Some Questions You Might Want To Ask

Being called sweetheart on the edge of sleep. The vulnerability of it, the trusting that there are no small knives hidden in the mattress.

Tractor trailers that fall over. Perhaps the driver, hot and sweaty, dircct from Fargo or Anchorage, grows drowsy and nods off, meanders his truck into your BMW. There's no question about what will happen, only the extent of the settlement your family can collect.

Nobody likes my lover; his combination of speechlessness and pushiness.hurts me every time I'm with him. I have decided to become a hermit until I can abandon him.

An old cliché: me on a silky blanket being fed mango slices and ice cream. Nude, of course, with a figure that compels admiration. Later, he paints my toenails fuchsia.

Listening to old voice mail messages. This may be illegal, so I shut all visible windows.

I chewed my braids as a kid. Now it's nails and ice cubes. How others react is a test of character.

Anything hot enough to make me sweat. The purge of spice and the worst that can happen is a bellyache.

My husband promised to take me fishing if I would bait my own hook. He used worms. In the twenty years of our marriage, we never went fishing. Too bad. Sitting there, quiet peaceful, waiting – this might have saved our marriage.

The call, the book, the Pulitzer, the kids I never had. The guy who loves me beyond imagination, etcetera. It's a long, long list.

And about the inside of my refrigerator? Neater than my soul. With some oddments: Nana's cranberry sauce, unopened; she died in '76. Blue-molded cheese. Miso soup mix I don't know how to use. Clotted buttermilk. Yes, definitely neater than my soul but not as fallen-to-pieces as my heart.

Last Morning on the Island

Morning whispers. Peewits
murmur in the hazels. Our bedroom
airs its linen, softened and rumpled
in six o'clock light, Christ on His cross
motionless, broken, a contrast to all
the winds and woods and pilgrim birds.

Church bells blister our ears,
remind us we're already late. Your face
folds into a stiff scowl, your voice
begins to smolder. We need
water from the creek. The weight of bottles,
large and small, hangs from our shoulders
in baskets. Blackberry cane
tears through our coats. We feel the air turn.

This is not the trail we should take.
This is not the fight we should be fighting.
Our voices escalate.
I conjure long steel scissors; you wrestle
the ropes that bind us. Our mouths
spray kisses while we hack and slash and struggle.

I'd rather be married to her than to me

even if stones were sticky with mud,
a stern wind kicking up the garbage cans.
Wine didn't pour until two then flowed all morning
and her shoes sounded like sunlight.
She rolled in the grass with him, in the sweet dew,
every morning an obsession sharp as coffee.
He saw Pasteur… Plato … DaVinci reflected
in her eyes when she looked at him,
the dining table littered with broken promises
and she never complained.

The wires went white with winter each year
and my car snowplowed its way to town.
So did hers. New tires (my money) – he jacked them on.
Her house bruised chaos and came out ahead;
my house ran like a little Swiss clock on high alert.
The cats grew constipated and got worms,
She ran up dresses on her little Singer, baked
loaves of bread that looked like bombs,
summer rain tasting of chocolate and ruby lips

while my angers rose in vapor from a noisy stove.
My favorite cat chewed on his privates,
my ass in New York, my head in Pennsylvania.
I drove a car crusted with crumbs.
The remains of a crow flapped from its antenna,
and I expected food in the cupboard, the mortgage paid,
squallering babies with time-off to nappy them,
a nod of appreciation to God and our parents
for our good luck, our brainy conversation: one good smack
in the chops of what used to look like love.

Hot Revenge

Let me find an axe
to chop down your house,
smash your trinkets,
trash your paintings,
pour oil over all the books
then set them alight
with a flourish.

Let me take a knife
to your newest lover,
poke an eyes out – yours
or hers – she can take it back
to Ohio, pickle it to give
to her relatives
for Christmas.

Let me dump a few files
from your computer,
post your password
on the Internet, divert
a few car payments
to my bank account.
I've earned it.

A Swim in Love's Angry Sea

Your fingers brush waves like prayers, your tongue's alive with only skin's salt and you smell the burning sheets. but you realize the house is not really on fire. It is the sea that is burning, truly burning, brine of sea water changing colors as the phosphorus glows. Then the house itself begins to catch fire so hot you taste the secrets in the rafters. You call "John" or "Richard" and your lover comes to you. Immediately from Cincinnati or Oakland he comes. But you do not understand the theory behind burning water so you cannot swim to the beloved to hand him his cell phone, his gigabytes of memory. You heave it to him, hear him yell, "Sell soybeans" to his broker. He has become the perfect president of mediocrity while swimming here. Clouds gather overhead; their fiery breasts suckle sea birds. Although you are sad, you abandon your lover to his gadgetry, and haul his lifeboat with you. When he notices, he waves, calls, "See you later, Jen," tells someone on the phone "she's a great girl" and you know he means you. He does not realize he will drown in this fiery ocean. He does not realize this is the point of this scabby poem. You know he will never understand the impediments of war, even if he is a victim of one. The ocean still burns, but you are no longer touched by it. A sip of wine – "Salud!" – and the wine bottle leaps to the table and pours itself. You do not mind anger but you are tired of swimming. You will check prices on boats built for power and speed.

Battle Music

We drive down the road fast enough to wag the fenders.
Jazz and Ferlinghetti blaze from WSGO's Morning Show
but we are mad, fighting mad, and we don't mean
to take prisoners.

We pass street lights blinking on and off.
We pass abandoned warehouses.
Further on, we pass a field of dandelions. We plan

to hit the stars with our darts and arrows because
we are very good shots. The missiles will ricochet.
We will annihilate each other.

The Beginning of the End

Rt. 80, the Poconos

Trees flash by on this February day,
tip of each branch a shaft of clear light.

I'd expected snow's white innocence
but brush all around glimmers bronze,
winter and not winter.

The gradual transparency
of tree limbs becomes our own.

We are translated into speech
of bone clothed in dying flames,
light flashing its semaphore,

our throats aching to speak but refusing,
the car heavy with words we'll never say.

The Circling of Gulls

You promise we will picnic at the cove
when gulls circle back to fish and scavenge,
say you will pack blankets and a wicker basket:
mangoes and brie, merlot nestled
in a burgundy napkin.

                          We'll eat the mangoes,
let their juices sketch rivers over the mounds
of our navels. You'll spill wine from your mouth
into mine, pat me dry with soft linen.
I will answer with my body.

You will take me beside the blue waters of the cove,
its changing shoreline, slip my blouse
from my shoulders, ease my pants past my knees,
lay me on sea-grass, succulent and shuddery
in the afternoon light.

……………………………………

In the real world, we pack blankets
and a wicker basket: crusty rolls and thin sliced ham.
We leave crumbs everywhere.
You tell me that once you loved a girl
and once you loved a woman
and I am neither.

                          We never notice
how the sun winks one immense eye, how minutely
light changes. Would a fool expect it to last,
even if it were possible? Errant gulls peck at the crumbs,
carry them away when their hunger overwhelms
this fractured world of sea and sky.

The Maine Coast

Last year,
I planned Thanksgiving snug in tree-clasp,
turkey among acorn trimmings,
oysters to stun the stuffing with their briny sap,
sweet tradition of rutabaga bitter in its bite.

November trees
stretched, full-leaved, over asphalt lanes,
ocean's roar and spume
barely hidden by underbrush and homes
or the small chaos of living.

I expected tobacco's blue haze,
football game bluster and bravo smoking the air,
both of us pushing bread
crumbs into the bird's clean hollow.
I expected the pumpkin pie to last and last.

I hadn't counted on the missing friend,
a small lost cat at the door, your sorry-stammer
that this wasn't love, not the way
you meant it to feel, that in this penetrating warmth
lay the boredom of content.

This year I go nowhere.
I watch branches unwrap outside my windows
and imagine coastal wind, fingers of fog,
the kitten weaving between my legs
as I set the table.

On the Red Wall

I can find a map of anywhere in the world I'd like to go
but I want to stay here, in your hallway. I can study
the calm architecture of your framed photographs:

the State House, the University Bell Tower, measure
the proportions of your mosaics or the Dadaist collage
you carried from Washington wrapped in a polo shirt.

If I lean toward your map, I can push pins into Chicago and
the Queen of All Saints school, the nuns who swatted you
when you asked where angels tucked their wings to sleep.

I can blow my breath over the waves of Lake Michigan,
the summers in the sun, Lansing and the slag heaps of
Detroit, Cleveland's smokestacks, Indiana's rolling fields:

your military marches through the corn. I can stick
a stamp on Alaska where your sisters lived for years,
or the little Spanish town hanging in the hills

behind San Francisco where you worked against the war.
How far south must I go before falling off the map,
before the Everglades slow suck, St. Augustine's decay?

I know this is the last kiss. I have pasted green sea glass to
mark the spot in Maine. Coastal waves break over my toes.
Wind's brave display blows leaves onto our slippered feet.

I'd rather plan for dirt to smear on Massachusetts,
mud mixed with cotton from the Worcester mills,
while I (oh, so carefully!) unpin my heart from the wall,

never moving from this spot. Some Salem witchcraft blows
smoke from hooked rugs underfoot, while I make this
the map that spells your life, your own red wall of fame.

Acknowledgments

Grateful acknowledgment is made to the journals that published the following poems, some in a slightly altered form: "The Mixed Gender of the Sea:" *360 Degrees*; "On the Red Wall," "Wolf:" *The Comstock Review.* "The Circling of the Gulls," "Gravel Roads:" *Louisiana Literature*; "Black Ice:" *The MacGuffin*; "Replacements:" *Mad Poet's Review;* "November:" *Mobius;* "Mangoes & Honey," " Desire:" *Monkey's Fist;* " The Maine Coast" (as "Thanksgiving at the Maine Coast:"): *Pearl;* "Varieties of Light:" *Poet Lore*; "The Beginning of the End," "How Your Hands Lay on My Skin," "Dark and Huge and Dusted with Wings:" *Poetry Depth Quarterly*; "In Times of Doubt," "Physical Examination:" *Poetry International*; "She Dreams of A Painting:" *Potpourri;*; "Twenty Years Apart:" *The Seasons*; "Battle Music:" *South Carolina Quarterly*

"Desire" and "Mangoes & Honey" (as "Lust") also appeared in *A Nickel Tour of the Soul* (FootHills Publishing, 2004).

Jennifer MacPherson lives in Syracuse, NY where she is Senior Editor of *The Comstock Review. In the Mixed Gender of the Sea* is her sixth full-length collection. Pudding House published her *Greatest Hits* in 2000 and a chapbook, *Stuck in Time*, in 2002. Published collections are *To Attempt A Tower, Another Use for Husbands, Cute & Perky, Slim & Sexy: A Poet's Guide to Personal Ads, As They Burn the Theater Down*. Her fifth full collection, *A Nickel Tour of the Soul*, is just out from FootHills.

A retired school psychologist, her work has recently appeared in *Poetry International, Louisiana Literature,* and *The Connecticut Review,* and is forthcoming in *South Carolina Review, The MacGuffin,* and *Pearl.* In 1993, she was named Syracuse's first Poetry Slam Champion. When away from her own poems, she can be found working for *The Comstock Review,* facilitating writing groups, whipping up gourmet feasts in the kitchen, or playing with her Burmese cats, Tillie and Muffit.